# SLANTWAYS

&#x266a; HEIDI COLTHUP

&#x266a; CLARE DAWES

&#x266a; PATRICIA DEBNEY

&#x266a; ABIGAIL EL-BEKAI

&#x266a; THOMAS PETER FINN

&#x266a; KATE L FOX

&#x266a; NANCY GAFFIELD

&#x266a; JOCELYN GODDARD

&#x266a; MARY GURR

&#x266a; EMMI ITÄRANTA

&#x266a; CHARMAINE JOSHUA

&#x266a; JENIFER KAHAWATTE

&#x266a; CHARLES PANKHURST

&#x266a; EMMA SMITH

*slantways*

AN ANTHOLOGY OF PROSE POEMS

edited by *Patricia Debney*
and *Jenifer Kahawatte*

WordAid.org.uk

First published in 2011 for WordAid.org.uk
by Categorical Books
70 Margate Road, Herne Bay, Kent CT6 7BH

For further information about this and other WordAid
projects, please visit www.wordaid.org.uk

ISBN 978-1-904662-13-6

A CIP record for this book is available from the
British Library

**All profits from the sales of this book go to the
JDRF (the Juvenile Diabetes Research Foundation,
Registered Charity Number 295716)**

dedicated to finding a cure

To order more copies, please send a cheque for
£9 per copy (including £1 postage & packing)
to Slantways at Yew Tree Cottage, Church Street,
Nonington, Dover CT15 4LD or visit www.wordaid.org.uk

*Saint Pancreas*, Oliver Double's stand-up comedy DVD
about diabetes, is available via *http://tinyurl.com/5tkax8x*
or *https://store.kent.ac.uk/browse/extra_info.asp?compid=1&
modid=1&deptid=1&prodid=59*

Printed in Great Britain by Lighting Source

# ABOUT THE JRDF

Type 1 diabetes – which is genetic and nothing to do with unhealthy lifestyles – means the pancreas can no longer produce insulin. Insulin is a hormone that allows the body to unlock the energy from the carbohydrates we eat. Without it, our bodies would become more and more clogged up with glucose and we would eventually die.

People with type 1 diabetes have to inject insulin or have it delivered into their body by an insulin pump. Balancing the insulin with the type and amount of food they eat (and exercise and illness and emotions and goodness knows what other factors) is a constant battle, and their blood sugars frequently go higher or lower than they should be. This can make them ill in the short term and have drastic effects on their health in the longer term.

I support the JDRF because both my children have type 1 diabetes. Tom – who likes cartoons and *Dr Who* and wearing suits and trilby hats – has been diabetic since he was under two years old, and he's eleven now. His older brother Joe, now fourteen – who likes indie music and science and Lego – was eight when he was diagnosed.

Founded twenty-five years ago by parents of children with type 1 diabetes, the JDRF is the world's largest funder of research into the condition. And the terrific thing about the charity is that its main aim is to find a cure. Currently it is funding research into the causes of diabetes, improving the equipment diabetic people use, and helping with long-term complications. In short, plenty to give the many kids like Joe and Tom hope for a better future.

*Oliver Double*
Senior Lecturer in Drama, University of Kent
**February 2011**

# FOREWORD

In November 2008 my then twelve-year-old son was diagnosed with type 1 diabetes. We rushed him to hospital on Wednesday, and I was due to teach my MA prose poetry module on the following Monday. Which was out of the question.

But the class happened anyway. Attendance was noted and they carried on – critiquing their prose poems and analysing handouts. They even wrote a report for me afterwards!

It was a special cohort, unfazed when I returned the following week and became tearful. And they produced glorious, risky, finely crafted work – both on that module, and beyond.

Last spring, over two years on, Jenifer Kahawatte approached me: the class and a few others wanted to put together a prose poem anthology in aid of JDRF. It turns out that her cousin is type 1, and since, former student Heidi Colthup's son has also been diagnosed.

It's an unfair world. But it's made bearable by understanding, by thoughtfulness – and by art. This anthology is broadly the product of that MA module, and a testament to the talent and commitment of its writers. If poetry looks at life from another angle, prose poems do it *slantways*, as the title suggests. Both inside and outside of form and convention, prose poems appear quite ordinary on the surface or page yet all the while wrestle with the unusual and extraordinary just beneath. Often surprising, often philosophical, prose poems both destabilise and satisfy. Despite being in constant tension, and juggling with so much, they work.

Which could also be said of living with a chronic condition like diabetes: invisible on the surface, and in constant, barely controllable flux underneath. 'Slant-ways' becomes second nature, becomes how you see and experience the world with all its variation, difference and unpredictability. Somehow, it has to work.

I am grateful to and ridiculously proud of the writers represented here – for their luminous writing, which in my view includes some of the finest examples of prose poetry around today, and for their lasting and unobtrusive kindness. I am particularly indebted to my fellow editor, Jenifer Kahawatte, for acting on the idea – and for doing the lion's share of the work! Also to Vicky Wilson for her copy-editing and production skills, and as always to Nicky Gould for the thought that became WordAid.

And to you. Enjoy. Give. It's worth it, in *every* way.

*Patricia Debney*
February 2011

# CONTENTS

# Heidi Colthup

lives in Kent and has a grand masterplan that involves reading books in bed while eating cake. But until that comes to fruition, she divides her time between writing and teaching.

'The Seahorse' was first published in *Shadowtrain*, Issue 26, November–December 2008.

## THE SEAHORSE

During the winter the seahorse stays inside, next to the hearth. He sits and grows his pregnant belly as his wife stokes the fire. Higher and higher the flames leap as he grows rounder and rounder. He knits seaweed bonnets while she reads seed catalogues. They do not move away from their farmstead for all of winter even though the rain lashes down and the plankton become wild with the storms for he has to be as calm as the very depths of the ocean in order to bring forth his shiny, warm offspring.

## SWALLOWS

At daybreak they are like black insects. I stand and watch their swooping in the sky back and forth from mud home to waterhole. Fluttering, arcing in the sky. My husband told me about the gobbets of mud they use to build their homes. He poured water into dusty pools for them. Lifting and wheeling, leaving their cloudy breath behind them, they build, mate, hatch, rear. At twilight they sing love songs to each other. The wind whistles around the empty rooms and comes back to slap me in the face. I pick up my suitcase and leave.

## BEACH BOYS

White bodies, red forearms, red feet, matching blue shorts, goggles perched on their heads. They dip and squawk in the rock pools. Their nets come up empty, no crab to nip at their plump pink toes, neat shell nails washed by sparkling bubbles of salty champagne.

Stout bodies wrapped in elderly coats with matching hats, bifocals perched on their noses. They watch the clouding horizon, sun lowering in the purpling sky, stars soon to twinkle. Their rough, reddened hands bitten by sea winds still find sand running through fingers.

# Clare Dawes

was born in December 1941 in Shanghai, China, and spent two-and-a-half years in a Japanese civilian prisoner-of-war camp. She is working on an extended family saga, but discovering prose poetry offered another challenging way to capture fleeting memories. 'Rain' and 'Wooden Stool' are part of a cycle entitled 'Fragments of Internment'.

# RAIN

*Itsy bitsy spider climbs up the water spout; down comes the rain and...*

day, after day, after day it rains. I clamber onto the upended camphor-wood trunk that someone has made into shelves, and look out of the window

nothing but rain. no children in the compound. no guards in the doorways. just a world full of raindrops

and I wait

# WOODEN STOOL

This is my stool, my little wooden stool that someone has made from the lid of the camphor-wood trunk. This is a box, my little wooden box, with bricks that just fit, that someone has made from the lid of the camphor-wood trunk. These are the tiny chairs and table for very small people that someone has made from the lid of the camphor-wood trunk.

I sit on my stool and I play with the bricks. I take the bricks out and I put the bricks in. I take the bricks out and I put the bricks in. I turn the bricks over and over and one side has letters that mummy calls ca-pi-tals and they make a rhyme that you can say over and over.

The sun comes out. I take my stool out and go to the place where the big children are sitting in rows. I sit on my stool and someone is talking but I can't under-stand, so I take my stool back into the hut and sit on the floor and the stool is a boat when it's upside-down

and mummy says one day we will go on a boat to a place where someone called grannie is waiting

# MUSICAL BOX

*Lot 169; early Victorian musical box, plain mahogany case*
*(4" x 3½" x 1¾"), small curved antique brass operating*
*handle; plays two tunes; some damage.*

Two turns of the cedilla-shaped handle and I am back
once more in my grandmother's house.

It is Sunday afternoon, and I sit turning the handle
slowly to hear each tune precisely three times, before
returning the box to its place.

I am a careful child, brought up to listen quietly to the
grown-ups, to sit on an uncomfortable hassock near
the open fire

to hear the hiss and spit of ash logs, to smell the
pungent scent of pine cones, to watch the crumpets on
the toasting fork

to know when to speak and when to be silent.

# CROWN DERBY COFFEE CUP

It was your favourite trinket, you said; you, who gave your medals to the Dayaks in Borneo when drunk, who never cared for possessions, who only had one tie (a knitted woollen one) when we met.

Yet that little cup and saucer appealed to you, with its design of sweet spring posies, the dimpled edge pressed as if by tiny fingertips on pastry, forming the faintest impression of a ring of dainty milkmaids joining hands around its circumference.

It never had a partner, stood on the small Welsh dresser with the china pig for company. Occasionally you picked it up, smiled, and replaced it carefully with a shrug.

A children's game of hunt-the-thimble and disaster struck; the cup seemingly shattered beyond repair. You would not blame the offending child, did not criticise the careless adult. You said nothing.

My mother gathered up the broken pieces, mended the cup with deft fingers. 'There,' she said triumphantly, 'as good as new!' But we would always be able to see the cracks in a certain light.

# HEAD AND HEART

I open a drawer and find your head – the head you
moulded with broad hands, a miniature replica I can
hold in my palm.

Look at the domed forehead, the Anglo-Saxon nose,
the determined chin reproduced in our daughters.
And I can see you, shoulders back, head high, striding
down the road smiling at your own internal thoughts,
a world apart.

Did you know it was your own image you were
creating with the children's modelling clay? Or that
I would stand here today remembering how my small
Celtic heart would skip for a moment when we met
unexpectedly in the street?

# *Patricia Debney*

teaches creative writing at the University of Kent. Her first book of prose poems, *How to Be a Dragonfly* (Smith Doorstop Books), won the 2004 Poetry Business Book and Pamphlet Competition. She wrote her forthcoming second collection, *Littoral Drift*, during a residency in a beach hut on the North Kent coast, eighteen months after her son was diagnosed with type 1 diabetes.

# ONSHORE WIND

In your own back garden, the sun bakes. New leaves unfold as you watch and tulips flood with high colour. The earth greens.

Here the seasons have different signals, and the tides repeat their complex but regular patterns regardless of temperature: diurnal, neap, equatorial, perigean. Algae bloom and fade, and barnacles cling and release, wash up in all weathers.

This is not about you. Or you. Or anything we might think responds to sun or shower, heat or cold, tenderness or neglect.

This blows a wind past you that was going to blow anyway. This sweeps sediment according to size and weight and deposits it further down the shore. This shapes whatever you do and have done.

You thought you had got to grips with the turning, tilting world, and your place in it. The vegetable pattern of growth and death, the length of the arcs of parts of this life.

But here there is more grey. And no beginning, no end.

## BREAKING

There is elegance in public drama. You curl, arch over like a dancer, plunge. The foam is clean white, short-lived, and dies, swooning, right at the feet of the shore.

Or tell no one. Reach the point where your legs buckle, pull out from under. Collapse. We've all done it. Only a few bubbles on the surface to show for it. When you can touch bottom again, stand up.

Or this morning. The long, slow spill. Posts shake in their moorings, flags whip back, and there is nothing you can do but feel it come in waves that topple way out to sea, and are dragged, still raging, head under, for metres more than you thought possible.

This happens only rarely, and requires certain conditions. A fast-rising tide, deceptive incline, relentless wind.

## MAKING WAVES

It's true we can ride most things out. We track them approaching and know we go up and over, brace ourselves for the drop. In clear water, we see them coming.

Only this is what happens: you rock the boat. You tip it from side to side and front to back, and believe me it feels dangerous.

My sea legs fail. I grab the edge, curl my fingers round the rim, imagine mouth to mouth. Battle through some freak storm.

Did you know one third of all waves are classed significant? Enough of them and you or me – one of us – goes overboard.

## CROSS WIND

On the other side of the spit, water rages, shoulders some submerged punching bag that never gives an inch.

While over here, the tide curls its lips, laps against the shore, stretches, as if resting.

This morning the wind has swung right around. Which makes a nice change, I admit.

# THIS TIME TOMORROW

Half an hour from this time tomorrow, you will go out onto the spit again. You will take each step as the water peels back.

You'll wade in, then watch your feet dry as the tide recedes. Move as far as you dare into the low waves rolling up the bank, see the light crystallise the eddies to almost solid, then watch them disappear.

You will find that the way opens out to you. That you will not be cut off and left for dead, your children crying for their mother, your husband scanning the horizon forevermore.

In so many ways, it's that simple. The more you walk here the more you know the tides, the play of wind and gravity, and land. The less you know you understand.

# Abigail El-Bekai

was born and raised in Abu Dhabi. She started turning her music into poetry when she first picked up a guitar at the age of eleven. She hasn't stopped writing since.

'How to Walk a Labyrinth' was first published in *Labyrinth Pathways 3*, July 2009.

# GARBAGE

i've been dumped. they shove garbage down my throat. i choke. 15 empty Walkers crisp packets, 1 Snickers wrapper, 2 Wispa wrappers, left-over chilli, gone-off milk, gone-off chicken, a bowl of something now unrecognisable from being infested by mould. the bowl crashes as it hits the bottom of my stomach. shards of glass pierce my lungs, my heart, my kidneys, my liver. i'm bleeding but they keep disposing: uneaten soggy cereal, 8 Quality Street wrappers, a 16-week-old Tesco value cheesecake, a jar of expired salsa, a tub of hummus, mouldy bread, mouldy cucumber, an untouched bowl of porridge: shove, shoved, shoving. i try not to speak, my putrid breath stinks the kitchen out so i stay mute forever, until they rake the rubbish out of my throat.

# HOW TO WALK A LABYRINTH

1.  Like everything else in life, there is one path which leads to an ocean of corridors. Do not be afraid to step onto the boulevard. It is natural to be frightened for many of us refrain from walking, unsure of where the trail might take us.

2.  In each of our minds there exists a jungle of avenues; it always leads to one place. Keep walking until you find it.

3.  In the labyrinth there is a clock. It clicks loudly. Do not count the seconds of every minute of every hour: this leads to days to weeks to months to years, spent on counting.

4.  Life is a bleak transit room. You either walk or wait or walk and wait. When you choose to walk, do not count your footsteps.

# THE PLATYPUS

*Boredom: the condition of being bored; ennui. Bored: (adj.) feeling tired and impatient because one is doing something dull or one has nothing to do.*

God must have been bored to tears when he created the egg-laying, semi-aquatic, venomous, duck-billed, beaver-tailed, otter-footed mammal whose existence scientists believed to be a joke. So the next time you step in dog shit, or you're having a bad day, think of the poor platypus, who belongs neither at land or at sea, whose face is stamped on the reverse of every Australian 20 cent coin to remind the world of its laughable existence.

# Thomas Peter Finn

was born on the Romney Marsh in 1987. He has
written for as long as he can remember and got the
opportunity to put this to good use at the University
of Kent. In his spare time Tom is an English teacher;
he currently lives in Ashford.

## MS STONE

Smells like coffee in the mornings. Smells like whiskey in the afternoons. All day Friday she smells like both. Our first lesson. She seems strict, sets rules, but can't keep a straight face. Waters her plants and talks to them like they're her children. We look at her. She looks back.

'You raise that eyebrow a millimetre further, I'll rip it off your face!'

She flicks her hair. Scoffs at us. She's like a child herself. I see her, hiding under the desk during a storm.

'You're never too old to be scared of thunder.'

When she's bored and we're supposed to be working, she insults us. None of us had done anything wrong. Ms Stone, are you trying to seduce me?

'My Dad could have your Dad in a fight.'

When Carl Miller's Dad got a job at the school as a caretaker, she took that back.

'There he is, waltzes in here, class starts at ten, struts in at ten past. Bit of scribbling here, bit of scribbling there. Go home, have a beer, relax. Chill. I ask you? Why bother?'

## WHY DOESN'T TRAVIS COME TO THE QUIZ ANYMORE?

Travis sits next to his window. A helicopter search-light blinds him. Landing in the garden. Travis runs outside. Jumps aboard. Between the stairs and outside he changes from grubby T-shirt into tuxedo. Inexplicable. Just like Travis. Dad runs after him. 'Your turn to do the washing up!' Travis shrugs, climbs aboard. Brad and Ange smile back at him.

'Thought you'd forgotten about us.'

'Well, I do normally have the quiz.'

Fly to the Swiss Alps. Expensive dinner. Brad excuses himself and Ange makes her move. 'Let's run away together, Travis!' A torrid love affair. Two months later. Travis in bed with Angelina, laying on his back.

'I'm sure they think I'm just being contrary and obnoxious, but I can't go to the quiz anymore. I'm just too busy.'

♪ ♪ ♪

Travis sits next to his window. This isn't about social politics. This isn't about fraying friendships. It's not about being contrary or obnoxious. This isn't about getting attention. This is about having better things to do.

## ROOT MENU

The music ends and repeats.

I come to life, still half asleep. It could be the early hours of the morning, or that someone else is up. If I left the volume on too loud, why have I only woken up just now?

The music ends and repeats.

I fumble in the darkness for the remote. The disc spins, round and round. The more I hear the music, the stranger it sounds. I don't like going to bed alone. This is why I leave it on.

The music ends and repeats.

The more I hear it, the stranger it sounds. The twisted ribbon of a cassette tape, or the distant cries of a man slowly drowning. Sometimes the music becomes unrecognisable. My restless mind has re-arranged the notes.

The music ends. I appreciate however much time I have left.

# Kate L Fox

enjoys writing poetry. She won a creative writing award while studying for her first degree at Anglia Ruskin University. The subject matter was 'the everyday' and the poem was about her local launderette.

'Addiction' was first published in the microfiction and prose poetry anthology *Exposure* (Cinnamon Press, 2010).

## ADDICTION

He rolled the carpet into a giant cigar and started
to smoke it. The shag pile burned well enough and
gave him a pleasant high. He defrosted the fridge
freezer and melted it down on a teaspoon. The kitchen
table and chairs broke up into powder that went
straight up his nose. He drank the three-piece suite.
The house finally empty, he started to pick at the walls
brick by brick.

## DETERMINATION

Marsupial babies don't grow to full size in the womb. In a typically gritty Aussie manner they think nothing of climbing to the pouch when they are still foetuses. I say 'good on ya' to the little blighters. These tiny koalas and kangas, born from their mother as red specks, crawl northwards through a forest of fur to find the pouch. They clamp onto a teat and drink milk in order to grow legs and arms, the kind of stuff we'd have got done first in the womb. But hey, that's pioneers for you.

## RUSTED POTENTIAL

The water gathers in a pool at your feet. It has been dripping continuously from your elbows and nose for some years now. Like the tin man who hasn't been oiled, your joints screech like startled parrots. Soon you will be frozen to the spot like a stranded turtle, hardly bothering to wave your flippers. Like your land-based cousin, you got left way behind and the hare can just be seen, a speck on the horizon, crossing the finish line.

## NOVEMBER

Picture this postcard scene. Frozen-pea green grass. Winter trees that have lost their leaves and stand naked. Watery warmth from the sun. An oast house in one corner and a church in the other, surrounded by bitter chocolate branches. The field is ribbed like a side of salted beef. The Garden of England has been sliced open and all the bruised fruit scooped out.

# THE CORE

A serene, candlelit hymn is being sung by the telly downstairs. Bonfire haze hangs like exiled cigarette smoke in the frozen air. The remains of the pheasant is becoming a soup. These aromas combine in my nose as I look out of the top window across the fields. The last of the pinkish grey light on the distant trees tells of ancient times when everything was just as it is now.

# Nancy Gaffield

was born in the US and has lived in the UK since 1990. She has published poems in *14*, *Magma*, and on the website *The Bow-Wow Shop*. Her first collection, *Tokaido Road*, will be published by CB editions in April 2011. These prose poems are part of a cycle entitled 'The Western Slope'.

## SOAP OPERA

Door ajar, safety chain fastened. I call and you turn from the screen and its trademark voice-over: *Like sands through the hourglass, so are the days of our lives.* Bathed in cathode blue, you are thinner. Frailer.

Salem's Christmas tree mysteriously catches fire and Marlena becomes possessed by demons. *Boy, she never saw that coming.* It took John Black twenty years to get his girl.

When it was over, we could talk, but they were all you'd talk about. That man Deveraux returned from the grave three times. You couldn't manage it once.

I fly back from Beijing to the house where you lived. The window-sill is lined with beer bottles, the door shut tight. A flicker from the TV seeps underneath, where someone, then no one, is waiting.

## GHOSTS, IN THE COMPANY OF

*I'll teach you to drive,* my father said, *on the road to Durango.* We head south on the strand along the eastern slope. Reluctant to rise from its cover of clouds, the sun slides into place like an egg on a plate. On our right the Rockies straightedge the distance from Denver to Raton Pass. The old undertaker dozes and I go on alone. Pedal to the metal till the wheel judders.

It's easy to drive. Snow-covered cone of Pike's Peak gawps in the wing mirror. Up we climb past the glacial waters of Lake Granby, a tiny clan heading into the back range.

At Durango we stop to refuel. I order Positive Dream of a Coconut Cream Pie. We eat like there's no tomorrow. *Lucky that box just fits,* he says. On the way back, the old man is snoring. Sun has switched sides. The passenger nudges the back of my seat: *Mommy, are we there yet?*

Best not to think of him in his suit of grey skin breathing or not just beneath my ribs.

# THE HOUR OF LEAD

In this cemetery on the edge of out-of-town, young trees unfold their rangy limbs. A coffin balances on steel over frozen ground; inside the hand of a woman holds a white gardenia. They've removed her glasses, her wedding ring. A small group casts the only shadow in argent light, sucking their fingers for warmth. *What a day for a funeral.*

Later the neighbours bring covered dishes. Tuck in. Meat loaf and oven-fried chicken. Four-cheese lasagne. Green jello salad. Squash and carrot casserole, washed down with cherry coke. Cakes and pies for after. There's a party atmosphere. Everyone's hugging and exchanging meaningful looks. *It was a good funeral.* I am given the glasses, the ring.

As if I'd been here before, I know what happens next. Aunt Wendy's youngest will drop his plate, cake-side down. Burst into tears. I wish I could cry like that. Throw myself belly-down and let 'er rip. Fill the room with the Black Sea. Instead, I put on my boots, go for a walk. The town at night is an imperfect vacuum, like deep space, where you are now.

Or did I just imagine that? Am I still on the sofa in a stupor between my brother-bookends?

# Jocelyn Goddard

finds experimenting with prose poetry a good distraction from writing fiction, which is currently her main interest. She is working on a novel set in 17th-century Oxford. These prose poems are part of a cycle entitled 'Mother–daughter' which was short-listed for the University of Kent T.S. Eliot Prize.

# PRIVATE VIEW

You went out with a painter for quite a long time; you learned how to sit. He was in between the guitar player (heavy metal) and the photographer (cityscapes). Then there was that fling with the break dancer and now you're in recovery from the one with a theatre company (great reviews, Edinburgh Festival).

Just experimenting with different art forms, you say, and we laugh and I say you could probably get an Arts Council grant for that...

then your eyes flick down and away and I'm thinking it could be the reference to money although it's probably just the lack of originality in that last remark and you look back up with the hint of a sigh still on your face but you say Tracey Emin comes to mind and I'm remembering that Saturday you came home from the shop and told me you'd sold her a pair of socks but I know it's her work that you're talking about and I say do you mean the one where she stitched all her lovers into her tent well I think she would be proud of you...

and anyway, even if she wasn't, I am.

## YOUR SECRET

In our family we do not buy pastry in packets or mixes
or kits. We consider that
- it makes cheap ingredients expensive
- it takes all the spontaneity out of your jam tarts

We thought we all knew how you did it. We managed
to pick up most of your technique, watching over and
over how
- the ball of dough chases loose pieces around the
  sides of the bowl
- the rolling pin keeps the rhythm: push, push, turn,
  push, push, turn

When we asked you for a recipe or looked for the
scales, you waved a vague arm. You always said some-
thing like
- it depends how much you need            or
- just keep on adding more until it looks about right

It takes a lot of practice to craft the perfect croute.
Sooner or later, we were bound to run into difficulties.
You would make comments such as
- it could be the weather            or
- maybe your hands are just too warm

Now no one in our family can remember when they
last tasted the comfort of your special pastry, which
was always
- slightly crisp
- crumbling softly
- not exactly sweet itself but holding sweetness in it

# WHAT SHE WOULD HAVE WANTED

Do not let them lay me out in polyester; nor wind me in a Terylene shroud; nor rest my poor empty head on a hypoallergenic memory-foam pillow. Make sure they do not encase me in an antique-finish MDF coffin with glossy acetate lining and lacquered brass-effect handles. Remember that for me there is no disrespect in sack, basket and spade.

Explain to them most politely that this is not simply a request for biodegradability – although a wooded hillside sounds a peaceful resting place and a willow-woven cradle, creaking quietly of its early days on the Somerset Levels, would be a fine last bed for me. Tell them how I always loved the feel of a silk scarf round my neck, of smooth Egyptian-cotton sheets and the smallest handkerchief of Liberty lawn.

See if you can find one of those muslin squares my mother used to lay across her shoulder under her babies' little faces; boil it to the softness that let her navy lambswool cardigan and starched white Peter Pan collar show through the weave; rinse it in cold lavender water and hang it on the breeze to dry; drift it in gentle folds over my heart.

Send me home the way I first settled into the world: in touch with the natural fibres of the Earth and wrapped around by love.

## 1. Analogy: More like B than A

### A. Bonding

A high-strength agent will produce the most effective seal when used to join articles composed of the same basic materials. If applied according to instructions, it will dry clear and without any obvious sign of treatment. Surfaces to be bonded should be clean and free of any potential contamination. Once the bond has completely set, it is sometimes found to be stronger than either of the items joined.

### B. Separation

You may find that individual plantlets can be gently teased out and pulled away. In other cases, you will need to lift the entire clump and divide it. The traditional way is to use two forks: thrust them both right into the middle, back to back. Then, using the handles as levers, force them apart. Once the plant mass begins to loosen, you will need to remove your gloves and disentangle the sensitive roots. The small outer pieces usually grow on vigorously once replanted. The older part, at the heart, may already be too woody to move.

## 2. Example

There is no more hot water. I pull out the plug and push myself up very slowly with a hand on each side of the bath. It is late. I have not had a whole night's sleep for eight weeks. You will be awake and crying for a feed again soon. I reach for a towel, twist round, turn my head over my naked shoulder to check out that bruise. Just over the hard lump at the site of the injection, it has been spreading and changing colour like a sunset over the sea. There is nothing there. Suddenly it hits me: I am looking on my body for the injury to yours.

# Mary Gurr

studied Fine Art at Brighton and at Byam Shaw School of Art in London and worked as an artist in Ireland before developing her interest in writing poetry and prose. She has published poems and been awarded prizes in the Kent & Sussex Poetry Society's Open and Folio competitions. She has two grown-up children and lives in Tunbridge Wells, Kent.

## THE WOMAN WHO SWEEPS

The woman who sweeps is going up the wall. Six a.m. and she is halfway up her ladder. Now that she has swept away all she can from the ground, she is reaching out to the brickwork.

She is really going at it.

The gutters will be interesting. I wonder if she knows how full of muck they are. She tries but they are too high. The weight of the broom nearly topples her.

She is concentrating on the here and now.

Hers are by far the cleanest walls around. From where I sit with my tea and egg, I can see a bird nesting in the hopper above her head. It's been there four weeks now. Every day I see her getting closer with that long, old brush of hers.

I see her lips move:

*Fly, damn you, fly!* she is hissing at the broom.

Or muttering incantations, mumbo jumbo – I could put any words I like into that hard, thin mouth of hers.

## THE PURPLE TREATMENT

The pigeons have performed again. It must have been a night drop from the sycamore that overhangs the car park round the back.

They steal the berries from the witch's garden, pulp them on the pergola and then in bold, Pollocky splodges, make art on my Mondeo.

I notice the witch's car never gets the purple treatment. I watch her snipping at her sloes as though she's amputating thumbs, the tip of her tongue just visible on her upper lip.

The pigeons lurk in blobs among the privet while she's operating – plump, grey gurglers, too heavy with the glut to bother further than required.

They must have come to some arrangement.

# NIGHT OWL

The owl has moved closer, into my elm. He is hooting
at me through my bedroom window.

I've been thinking about him a lot lately, wondering
what he's really like under that feather.

At midnight my cuckoo clock calls back at length
but I don't think he can hear it, though he might be
pretending.

I only saw him once, when he flew in front of some
clouds lit up by the moon. At least I think it was him.

He keeps me from sleep most nights, for a while.
Maybe I'll miss him when he goes back to the woods,
maybe not.

I don't know what his intentions are.

# LUCK

A midnight dash, two of them, tearing up the middle of the road.

I envy the lope of the vixen. Her sprint is fast and light, eager, she's ahead by several lengths. She's very young.

They're heading for the park, an ideal spot, private and old. Thousands of lives have started in there. They may even be related.

At the gate she stops and looks at him, only for a second. The stiff-backed old dog fox can hardly believe his luck. I can see his tongue.

Could be she thinks he's after food – a normal night – or wants to play.

She can't believe her luck.

Her screams are long and difficult to interpret.

They fluctuate.

# DEAD DOG CORNER

Down there is where I killed the dog.

It wasn't my fault. It ran out of the hedge, darted in between my wheels. There was a flash of white –

It just ran out.

Its squealing filled the road, filled my head. It was rolling around, its stomach burst open like –

It just ran out.

Its owner was so mad – not with me, with the dog – for getting itself killed I suppose, only it was still alive –

*It just ran out*, I said.

The owner was shaking the dog like he was trying to teach it a lesson. *Fucking dog*, he was saying –

But the dog and its stomach –

just ran out –

And he was dragging the half-dead dog out of the road and in the gate –

# Emmi Itäranta

grew up in Finland and has explored different forms of writing from drama to journalism. She often spends more time with fictional characters than with real people, currently works as a columnist for a Finnish newspaper and completed her first novel in 2010. She has no plans to stop writing anytime soon.

# ARCTIC SPECIES

## Ice Bat

Only visible to the naked human eye during the brief moment between day and night, its crystal wings will cut through the translucent sheets of Arctic air before night forges a blind armour on its shape and we might as well look away.

Its blood will darken once spilled. People have been known to travel from afar to admire the bruised purple against pure snow. Weapons are not needed to create such a sight: an ice bat is so fragile it can be shot down with a glance, its spine snapped and splintered without a word. A single sharp thought will suffice.

## Giant Snow Lemming

If you see one, do not be alarmed. It cannot see you. Its natural ignorance of a world beyond its own has made it the dominant species in the Arctic. Unable to perceive any real enemies, it spends its life fighting imaginary ones. This keeps potential predators from approaching it.

Another theory suggests that the giant snow lemming itself is, in fact, an imaginary creature, and therefore virtually indestructible.

# Nival Lynx

Their fur is the stuff of stories: soft as a kitten's belly, frost-coloured and brush-stroked with pale grey and the rarest limpid blue.

Only the eyes of another collector will recognise your perfect crime when you walk into the room. They will stick to it like a moist tongue to frozen metal. You let their gaze linger just long enough, and when you turn, you can sense the taste of blood in the gaping juice-red mouth, and in your own, dark and glistening like victory, more pungent than guilt.

## Fell Raven

They gather around you when you sleep, soundless inside their frost-white feathers. They wait, closer than you think, their bony beaks turned towards you.

By the time you open your eyes, they are gone, swept to the snow-spilled skies. The moment sleep pulls you in, they return, quiet and nearer than the night before.

Some say they are watching over your soul. Others, that they have come to take it away.

Even if you could ask, they would not answer.

## Polar Turtle

They sleep deep in the wrap of water, the slow-motion swim of their limbs keeping them afloat. The coarse arcs of their shells fit the invisible dents in the underbelly of the glacier.

If you press your ear to the ice, you may hear the distant clatter as the ocean rocks them against their underwater landscape.

They cannot tolerate daylight: it scorches them to ashes. If the ice grows too thin, they blaze and burn and sink.

Where one has died, you will first see a cave opening, wound-like. Then you will see water bleeding through.

You will barely have time to close your eyes before darkness washes over you.

# Charmaine Joshua

used to practise law but now writes for real. She is a former co-winner of the Decibel Penguin Prize and her short memoir, *Of Mango Trees and Monkeys*, was published by Penguin in 2007. She is currently working on her first novel.

## EVE AND MADONNA

In the still of the night, she comes when he calls. His cry rises as she nears and he smells the flooding in her breasts, engorged and dripping. He roots, desperate, as she fumbles, her fingers clumsy with fatigue. Fists flailing, mouth mewing, head lolling, nuzzling, probing, until with a quick hot stab, he latches. His cheeks pump, her milk flows, his body melds into hers, and all is calm again. Deep below, she feels another clamp and flow, an ancient lunar tide.

For a time she is both Garden of Eden and the Promised Land. Her womb weeps blood, but her breasts overflow with milk and honey.

## STORY TIME

When the older ones were away at school and the washing blew up on the line, she would gather me upon her lap with a dog-eared book and read. She smelled of soap and something sweeter, and her voice flowed into my ear, rising and falling, curling then crashing then curling again, filling me up and carrying me away. I turned my head and watched her mouth in wonder.

Later the others returned and reclaimed her one by one with their scratched knees and soaring hunger, while I, left alone to play, would watch her mouth pucker and scold and smile as she bandaged the bruises and ladled out soup, and recall the time when an ocean streamed out from it on which I sailed alone.

# CHERRY ON THE VINE

*Cherubino: grown exclusively for Waitrose in southern Sardinia, ripened on the vine until they reach their peak of sweetness, these are perfect in salads or simply roasted whole.*

You glistening orbs of beauty, little moons of blood, you lie nestling so chastely next to each other, as if butter wouldn't melt… Cherubino? Ha!

Your vines splay out like lizards' legs across your skin, their feet suckered to you in stars. Under the stars I find mud. But what could I expect from one who grows so close to the ground? How could you escape corruption?

You suckled from a soil soaked in the blood of conquest, an island lusted after and ravished. Or should I say ravaged? Passed from one invader to another. A trophy, a toy.

All this you imbibed. You know how to seduce. The juice of the apple runs through your veins. So don't play the virgin with me.

You fit so neatly in my palm, it's such a shame. I fold my fingers and gently squeeze, then suck your seeds from between the cracks.

# Jenifer Kahawatte

has a degree in philosophy and has worked in computing and taught in primary schools. Having co-written and performed in fifteen amateur pantomimes, she decided to develop her creative writing skills when she retired. She enjoys writing poetry, dancing, being a grandmother and had a poem published in the *Bridport Prize Anthology*, 2008.

## THE DIAGRAM PRIZE

*(awarded to the oddest of odd book titles)*

## The Joy of Chickens

The Rhode Island Reds are holding a hen party.

Cluck and scratch. Scratch and cluck.

Buff Orpingtons, Black Minorcas, Blue Silkies, Silver-Laced Wyandottes have dusted off their feathers.

Free-range. New-laid.

The Little Red Rooster struts his stuff.

## How to Avoid Huge Ships

- Steer clear of Fawley and Milford Haven.

- Don't leave harbour unless you really have to. Keep to the backwaters, creeks and broads.

- Try the local gravel pit or disused quarry to float your boat.

- Push a punt out on the Cam; take along your picnic hamper. Drift.

## Highlights in the History of Concrete

In my heyday I was the darling of Brutalist architects from Boston City Hall to the South Bank to a multi-storey car park near you. But how about Grandpa's crazy paving, or that bollard outside Aldi that collects new paintwork daily?

Splendid!

I'm not everyone's favourite, but I get around.

# A Pictorial Book of Tongue Coatings

*What is your taste in tongue coatings?*

Let us help to reveal the true you. (Beware of false imitations.)

This season's must-have colours are snot green and purple bruise (see p3). Into body-piercing? You may incorporate a stud of your choice into the design (see p5).

For smokers we recommend our faux-fur animal prints in nicotine brown patterned with bile black for a striking finish (see p8). They come in a choice of endangered species: cheetah, leopard or ocelot.

Over-sixties will love our new pastel collection (see p13). Bored with your usual blue rinse? Choose peach, rose or lavender. Why not ask your dentist for toning dentures?

For the young-at-heart we have our fabulous range of tartans and polka dots (see p16). All come with a choice of flavours (see p21). How about butterscotch, pear drop, dolly mixture?

*What does your tongue say about you?*

# Versailles: The View from Sweden

Screw up your imagination and look sideways to bring the image into focus.

Beyond our clean Scandinavian lines, minimalism, pure colour, raw herring, long winter nights, you may see on the horizon Gallic decadence, gilt mirrors, painted ceilings, draperies, Marie-Antoinette in her summer-house eating cake.

## Charles Pankhurst

has been published in *Logos* and *First Time* magazines as well as being both long-listed and short-listed for the Canterbury Festival Poet of the Year award. He lives in the Medway Towns where he makes the occasional open mic appearance at poetry readings.

# ONE IMPOSSIBLE THING
# BEFORE BREAKFAST

Morning time and the cats that aren't mine are waiting to be fed. One is on the window ledge looking in, pressing her little spiv nose to the glass. Her more aloof sister sits on the chair, her lime-lemon eyes inscrutable. Itinerants of the fur persuasion with their hard-luck meows, they are using their cats' wiles to psych me into feeding them. They know a soft touch when they see one. I feed them, enjoying the sound of their food being crunched into oblivion. I walk into the garden. It's the first decent spring day. One of the cats darts past and catches the first butterfly of the year, a peacock.

A velvet russet and blue wafer protrudes from her mouth, like some strange communion. Somehow, with a wing of twig and leaf, I distract the cat and she drops the butterfly. I pick it up and hold it in my cupped hands, send it healing, plea bargain with the universe for it to live. It trembles, I assume in its death throes. I open my hands and the butterfly stands tall, resurrected, flexes itself and takes off on a wing and a prayer, a fluttering kaleidoscope of colours over the gardens, for a moment the most majestic of creatures in this fierce-fragile world. The beat of its wings threatens to break my heart against the wheel of the sun.

# PULLING THE CURTAINS AT MIDNIGHT

The moon? A 50-watt bulb caught in black lingerie beams diffidently through a negative sky, highlighting inky spectres, cloudy changelings in constant metamorphosis.

The form of a cat, legs on different slats, lame-walks the fence in drunken deliberation then melts into the darkness.

Dolly pegs and forgotten clothes dance on next door's line. A sweater lays a protective arm over a fretful pair of socks.

On the terraced houses clay-pot cannon threaten the universe. Inside, families nest and fledgling dreams awake. A few windows smoulder yellow, becoming light pockets on the coat of midnight.

All in a moment the change-face traveller slips its dark chains and torches the sky burnished gold.

## SO THIS IS DEMOCRACY

The very early 21st century.
Baghdad.
A house.

The house is a mess.
NO – I mean a real mess.

Inside somewhere a family is dying. Under the rubble,
the father, in a clown's face of dust, slowly suffocates.
His wife is already dead. In a bedroom, now mostly
al fresco, their daughter lies, like a large rag doll among
the ruins.

They never got to vote.

# *Emma Smith*

loves to participate in any type of creative writing whenever the opportunity arises and regardless of whether or not it's appropriate. This is her first attempt at prose poetry.

# ELEPHANT

There is an elephant in this room. If it only stood there, indented the carpet a little, it would not be so difficult to bear. But this elephant is bringing the house down. This shrivelled, relentless beast trampling all that has been accumulated here, grinding it under toes that should really only walk across butter.

## THE APPLICANT

Still hard to believe that you would pour your smiles right into my face, force-feed me your enthusiasm and shake and shake my hand, and all the time you knew what you were going to say.

## TECHNOLOGICAL ASSISTANCE

Push myself down the stairs. I have been shocked out
of sleep by the shrieking panic of the telephone. Also,
the printer burbles in a stupor – help me. Help me.
Help me. I'm not sure what it is that they want me to
do for them.

Lightning Source UK Ltd.
Milton Keynes UK
22 February 2011
168044UK00001B/18/P